Look Inside a
Rock Pool

Louise Spilsbury

company incorporated in England and Wales having its registered office at 7 Pilgrim Street, London, EC4V 6LB – Registered company number: 6695582

www.raintree.co.uk
myorders@raintreepublishers.co.uk

Text © Capstone Global Library Limited 2013
First published in hardback in 2013
Paperback edition first published in 2014
The moral rights of the proprietor have been asserted.

Edited by Rebecca Rissman, Dan Nunn, and John-Paul Wilkins
Designed by Steve Mead
Original illustrations © Capstone Global Library Ltd 2013
Illustrations by Gary Hanna
Picture research by Ruth Blair
Production by Alison Parsons
Originated by Capstone Global Library Ltd
Printed and bound in China

ISBN 978 1 406 25129 6 (hardback)
16 15 14 13 12
10 9 8 7 6 5 4 3 2 1

ISBN 978 1 406 25136 4 (paperback)
17 16 15 14
10 9 8 7 6 5 4 3 2 1

British Library Cataloguing in Publication Data
Spilsbury, Louise.
Look inside a rock pool.
577.6'99-dc23
A full catalogue record for this book is available from the British Library.

We would like to thank the following for permission to reproduce photographs: iStockphoto p. 14 (© Amy Riley); Naturepl pp. 7 (© Ernie Janes), 8 (© Wild Wonders of Europe / Lundgren), 9 (© Gary K. Smith), 12 (© Philippe Clement), 17 (© Florian Graner), 19 (© Solvin Zankl), 21 (© Alan James), 23 (© Christophe Courteau), 25 (© Sue Daly), 26 (© Robert Thompson), 28 (© Simon Colmer); Photoshot p. 27 (© NHPA); Science Photo Library pp. 13 (ALEXANDER SEMENOV), 15 (FRED WINNER/JACANA); Shutterstock pp. 5 (© Wesley Cowpar), 6 (© Stephen Aaron Rees), 11 (© Martin Fowler), 20 (© nanadou), 24 (© vilainecrevette), 29 (© Juriah Mosin); Superstock p. 18 (© F1 ONLINE).

Cover photograph of starfish resting on a rock with seaweed, snails and barnacles in a tidal pool on Cape Cod Massachusetts, reproduced with permission of iStockphoto (© Amy Riley).

We would like to thank Michael Bright and Diana Bentley for their invaluable help in the preparation of this book.

Every effort has been made to contact copyright holders of any material reproduced in this book. Any omissions will be rectified in subsequent printings if notice is given to the publisher.

Disclaimer

Contents

Some words are shown in bold, **like this**. You can find out what they mean by looking in the glossary.

At the top

A rock pool is a pond on the **seashore** that fills with seawater. A **habitat** is a place where animals find **shelter** or food. We find some animals at the top of rock pool habitats.

A limpet is a sea snail with a hard, pointed shell. It clings to rocks so waves don't wash it away. It moves around to eat seaweed that grows on the rocks.

▲ Limpets can often be found in rock pools.

An oystercatcher is a **sea bird** with a long, red beak. Oystercatchers fly down to eat animals such as mussels in the rock pools.

▼ Oystercatchers watch rock pools for food.

▲ This oystercatcher is eating a mussel.

Oystercatchers use their strong beaks to push limpets and other shells from the rocks. Sometimes they smash shells on rocks to open them. Then they eat the juicy animals inside.

Shore crabs also come to rock pools to feed. They walk sideways over rocks and seaweed looking for small or dead animals to eat. They catch their lunch with their big **pincers**!

▼ Crab pincers are hard and strong!

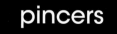

pincers

▲ Crabs can be difficult to spot in a rock pool.

Shore crabs are the same colour as the rocks and seaweed. This helps the crabs to hide from hungry **sea birds** that try to eat them.

On the rocks

Some creatures live in rock pools where they stick to one rock and stay there all their lives. Others move around on the rocks looking for food.

Dog whelks hunt limpets and other animals with shells. They use their sharp tongues to drill holes into the shells of their **prey**. Then they suck out and eat the animal inside.

Dog whelks have ▶ small, pointed shells.

Mussels have two shells that can close tightly together. They grow and live together in groups on rocks. Each mussel makes sticky threads to fasten itself to rocks.

▼ Mussels close their shells when out of water.

▲ Mussels open their shells when under water.

Mussels open their shells to eat tiny bits of food floating in the water. They stick out a tube and suck in water. Then they eat the food and spit the water out!

Starfish have five arms with tiny suckers underneath. These suck on to rock and seaweed so starfish can move around a rock pool and find food.

▼ Starfish can grow a new arm if they lose one.

▲ This starfish has wrapped up a meal!

The starfish uses the suckers on its arms to open shells. It pushes its stomach into the shell and around the animal inside. Then the starfish **digests** its **prey**.

In the water

Some animals swim around under water in the rock pool. They may move from pool to pool to find **shelter** or food.

Female lumpsucker fish lay their **eggs** in rock pools. The **male** fish uses a strong sucker on his belly to stick himself to a rock near the eggs. He keeps them safe from starfish and crabs until they **hatch**.

▲ Lumpsucker fish can suck on to rock!

Prawns have ten legs that help them swim and walk on rocks. The front legs have **pincers** for grabbing food. Prawns eat anything from seaweed to tiny bits of dead animals.

▼ Prawns kick their legs to swim.

▲ Prawns are good at hiding in rock pools.

Prawns are almost see-through. This makes it hard for hungry fish to spot them! Prawns also hide under seaweed to keep out of sight.

A gunnel is a long, thin fish with marks on its back that look a bit like eyes. The marks can fool **predators** into thinking the gunnel is a much bigger fish than it is, so they leave it alone.

▼ Gunnel fish twist and curl to swim.

▲ Gunnels often hide among plants.

The gunnel wriggles like a snake through the water. It swims down to the bottom of the rock pool and looks for worms hidden in the sand to eat.

Rock bottom

There are some very interesting animals living at the bottom of the rock pool, too.

A sea slug uses the two feelers by its mouth to feel its way around the bottom of the rock pool. It uses the two **antennae** on top of its head to smell out food to eat.

feeler

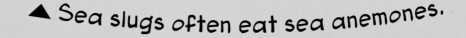
▲ Sea slugs often eat sea anemones.

Sea anemones look like strange flowers stuck to rocks, but they are animals. They wave their long **tentacles** about to catch food from the water.

▼ Sea anemones are meat-eating animals.

tentacles

▲ This shrimp is hiding from **predators.**

An anemone stings **prey** with its tentacles to make it still. Then it pulls it into its mouth. Some animals use anemones for protection. They hide among the anemone's tentacles.

Sea urchins move using suckers like starfish. They also have spikes which help to push them along. When they find seaweed, they scrape it up and eat it with the teeth under their shell.

▼ A sea urchin's shell is covered with spikes.

▲ This sea urchin has seaweed on its spikes.

The sharp spikes stop some animals eating sea urchins. Sea urchins also catch stones and seaweed on the spikes which help to **camouflage** them from **predators**.

Rock pool tips

All rock pools are different, but most are full of colourful and exciting animals. Sit quietly by a rock pool and watch carefully. What can you see?

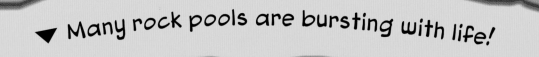

▼ Many rock pools are bursting with life!

▲ It is important to stay safe while you explore.

Have fun at rock pools but remember:
- Be careful what you touch because some animals can sting or nip.
- Only remove empty shells from the water.
- Take care walking over slippery rocks on the **seashore**.
- Watch out for waves and rising seawater.

Glossary

antennae (singular: antenna) thin parts on the heads of some animals, including beetles and lobster, that are used to feel and touch

camouflage cover or disguise that helps something blend in with its background and makes it hard to see

digest change food into substances that an animal's body can use for energy and to stay healthy

egg object produced by a female animal that can develop into or contain a growing young animal

female sex of an animal or plant that is able to produce eggs or seeds. Females are the opposite sex to males.

habitat place where particular types of living things are likely to live. For example, polar bears live in snowy habitats and camels live in desert habitats.

hatch come out of an egg

male sex of an animal or plant that is unable to produce eggs or seeds. Males are the opposite sex to females.

pincer body part made of two moveable, sharp pieces that can grasp things

predator animal that hunts and catches other animals for food

prey animal that is caught and eaten by another animal

sea bird type of bird that normally lives by the sea, such as gulls or oystercatchers

seashore land at the edge of the sea or ocean which is usually rocky or sandy

shelter place that provides protection from danger or bad weather

tentacles long, thin body parts of some animals, used to feel around them so they can find or capture food

Find out more

Books

Along The Shore (Oceans Alive), John Woodward, Franklin Watts, 2009

Coastal Treasure Hunter, Louise Spilsbury (A&C Black, 2010)

Seashore (Eyewitness), Steve Parker (Dorling Kindersley, 2011)

Websites

Find out more about rock pool animals at:
http://www.bbc.co.uk/nature/habitats/Tide_pool

This video is all about life in a rock pool:
http://www.bbc.co.uk/learningzone/clips/rockpool-animals/7518.html

You can do a tide pool puzzle or jigsaw at this site!
http://kids.nationalgeographic.com/kids/games/puzzlesquizzes/tidepools-puzzler/

Index